Contents

What is energy?

Energy is a power that makes things happen. Energy makes lights shine brightly and fires give out heat. Energy makes your body work. Without it, you couldn't think or run, and your heart would be lifeless and still.

Your body uses energy every moment of the day and night.

Save the Planet

Save Energy

Claire Llewellyn

Chrysalis Children's Books

First published in the UK in 2003 by
Chrysalis Children's Books
64 Brewery Road
London N7 9NT

ISBN 1-84138-692-8

British Library Cataloguing in Publication Data
for this book is available from the British Library.

A Belitha Book

Editorial Manager: Joyce Bentley
Senior Editor: Sarah Nunn
Design: Stonecastle Graphics Ltd
Illustrations: Paul B. Davies
Picture researcher: Paul Turner

Printed in China

10 9 8 7 6 5 4 3 2 1

Picture credits:
Corbis:
pages 4 © Michael Neveux/Corbis, 18 © Charles
O'Rear/Corbis, 19 (below) © Lester Lefkowitz/
Corbis.
Garden & Wildlife Matters Photo Library:
page 7 (bottom right).
Roddy Paine Photographic Studios:
pages 4-5, 8 (left), 14-15, 16 (left), 26-27, 29.
Sylvia Cordaiy Photo Library:
pages 19, 25 (above).

A freezer uses energy ▶
to keep our food cold
and fresh.

This fire burns coal to
release energy that
gives us heat. ▼

Where does energy come from?

Most of the energy we use comes from **fuels**, such as coal, oil and gas. When fuels are burned, they give off energy. This energy can be used to power all sorts of machines or to make **electricity**.

Oil, coal and gas are known as **fossil fuels**. They are made from plants and animals that died millions of years ago.

▲ Oil rigs drill oil and gas from rocks on the sea bed.

Power stations burn oil, gas and coal to make electricity. ▼

Electricity is a kind of energy. It can be wired to wherever it is needed. ▼

Global warming

When fuel burns, it gives off **carbon dioxide** – a gas that mixes with the air. Carbon dioxide traps the Sun's heat and is making our world warmer. This is known as **global warming**.

Smoke and **fumes** contain a gas called carbon dioxide. Every time we burn fuel, or light bonfires, we produce more and more carbon dioxide.

Global warming is upsetting the world's weather. To stop it, we need to burn less fuel and use energy much more carefully.

Global warming is causing more floods and violent storms.

Global warming brings heatwaves and droughts. Food crops wither up and die.

Using energy at school

Electricity provides energy at the end of a wire. We use electricity in all sorts of places, such as hospitals and schools. But take a look at this picture of a school. Is the energy being wasted?

Ordinary light bulbs use a lot of energy.

The hot taps are left running. The water was heated by electricity.

The classroom windows don't close properly so all the heat is escaping.

The hall has a very high ceiling. It takes more energy to heat the room.

This room is empty but the lights are on.

The corridors are empty most of the time, but they are as warm as the classrooms.

A better way of using energy

We can't stop using electricity but we can try to use it more wisely. Look at the picture below. Can you see how this school is helping to save energy?

Special energy-saving light bulbs use less energy than ordinary bulbs.

Store rooms have timer switches. The lights turn off after three minutes.

The taps are all turned off properly.

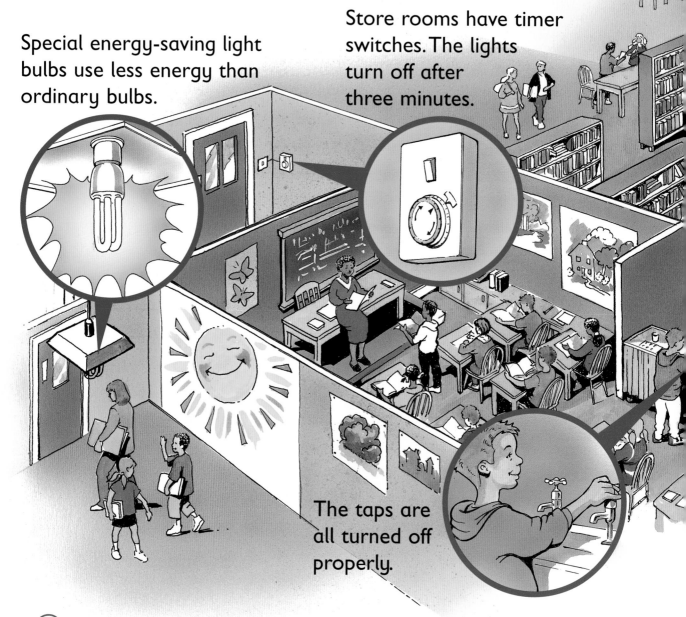

The windows close properly. This stops heat escaping.

The heating has been turned down in the corridors.

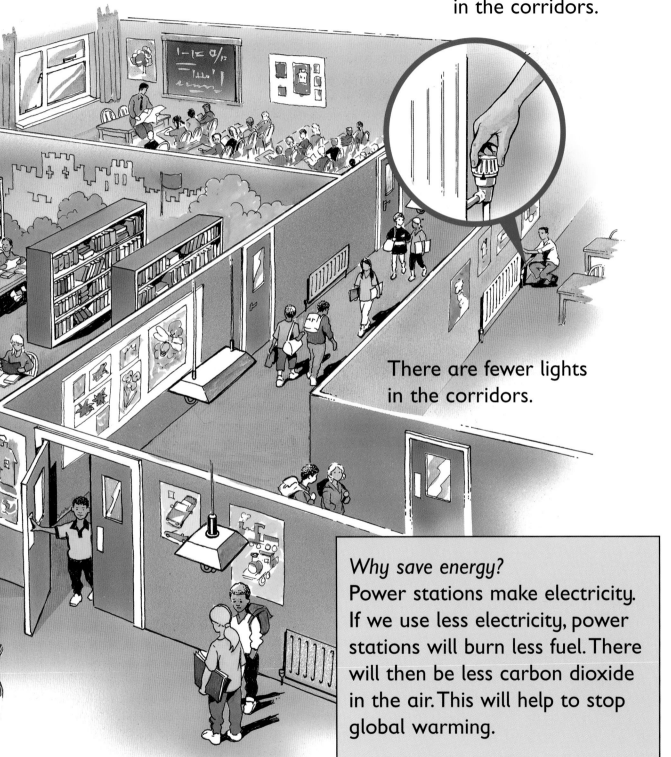

There are fewer lights in the corridors.

Why save energy?
Power stations make electricity. If we use less electricity, power stations will burn less fuel. There will then be less carbon dioxide in the air. This will help to stop global warming.

Saving energy in the home

We use a lot of electricity in our homes.
Every time we switch on the television or
the kettle, carbon dioxide is added to the air.
We need to think carefully about the electricity
we use if we want to stop global warming.

◄ Always fill up dishwashers
and washing machines before
you use them.

Always use a plug when you
run hot water into a wash basin
or sink. ▼

Always ▶ remember to turn off the lights when you leave the room.

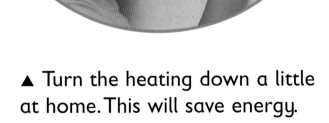
▲ Turn the heating down a little at home. This will save energy.

It takes electricity to keep a ▶ fridge cold. Always close the fridge door quickly so that cold air can't escape.

Recycling saves energy

Recycling is another way of saving energy.
Many of the things we throw away – old
newspapers, glass bottles and metal cans –
have been made using lots of energy.
Don't throw away these useful materials –
recycle them instead!

Don't throw
away glass
bottles – they
are easy to
recycle.
Recycling uses
less energy
than making
glass from
**raw
materials**.

Throwing away cans is a waste of all the energy that was used to make them. By recycling them you are helping to save energy.

Recycled goods take less energy to produce. Buy them whenever you can.

Looking at transport

Cars, buses, planes and trains need energy to move. This energy comes from fuels, such as petrol, which give off carbon dioxide. We can save a lot of energy if we think about transport and use our cars more carefully.

All vehicles give off fumes as they burn fuel. This adds to global warming and also **pollutes** the air.

There are many millions of cars in the world. Most cars carry very few passengers. This is a poor use of fuel.

Trains and other kinds of **public transport** make good use of fuel. This is because they carry so many passengers.

Getting around

We all use cars to get around – but cars are a very poor use of energy. Look carefully at this picture of a town. Can you see how energy is being wasted? What other problems can you spot?

Cars burn petrol and give off fumes.

Many people are going into town by car. Now there is a traffic jam and none of them can move.

This bus is nearly empty. Like the cars, it is burning fuel.

The more we use our cars, the more petrol we need to buy.

School children are being picked up by car. There are just one or two to every car.

Traffic fumes spoil the **environment** and add to global warming.

A better way to get around

We can't stop using our cars but we can all try to use them less often. Look at the picture. Can you see how energy is being saved? What has happened to the streets of the town?

A school bus is carrying lots of children. This saves parents from using their cars.

Some children are cycling to school with an adult. Others are walking.

Some people have left their cars at home and are taking the bus. This is a better use of fuel.

The less we use our cars, the less petrol we need to buy.

These people are sharing a car with their friends. They have left their cars at home.

Bikes are good for short journeys. They are quick, clean and easy to park.

There are fewer cars on the roads. It's much nicer to walk around the town and the air is cleaner, too.

23

Other kinds of energy

Oil, coal and gas won't last for ever. One day they will run out. Before they do, scientists are trying to make electricity from **natural** kinds of energy, such as the Sun, wind and flowing water. Natural energy is clean and safe, and does not lead to global warming.

The Sun's energy gives us heat and light. **Solar panels** use sunlight to heat water in a house.

◄ There is plenty of energy in the wind. **Wind turbines** use it to make electricity.

There is ► energy in running water. This **dam** contains machines that make electricity. They are powered by the running water.

Small actions, big results

Is it possible for you to save energy? Of course, it is! If your small steps are copied by millions of people, the results for the Earth will be huge! Everyone on Earth shares the planet. Everyone can help to save it.

What would happen if everyone used bikes more?

There would be fewer cars on the roads.

We would burn less fuel.

This would stop global warming.

What would happen if everyone used electricity wisely?

Homes, schools, hospitals and offices would all use less electricity.

Some power stations could be closed down.

This would cut global warming.

What would happen if most of our rubbish was recycled?

Factories would recycle materials rather than make goods from scratch.

They would use fewer raw materials.

They would use less energy.

Over to you!

No one wants the problems of global warming. Why not try one of the ideas below, and help to save energy?

Guess how many electrical machines you have in the house. Now, walk round your house – both inside and out – and count them. Were you right?

Every home has an electricity **meter** to measure the energy it uses. Ask an adult to show you yours. How much electricity do you use every week?

Talk to your parents about how you could all save energy at home. They should be interested – it will save them money!

Suggest to your parents that they fit energy-saving light bulbs.

Think of slogans to encourage people to save energy. Make posters to put up at home or in your school, local library or club house.

Do a survey to find out how people in your class come to school in the morning. Perhaps some of you could walk together or share a lift?

Investigate the way your school uses energy. Make and display stickers to remind people to save energy.

Keep a diary of the number of times in a week your family uses the car. Perhaps your parents could save fuel by combining several short journeys into a longer trip.

Suggest that everyone in the family has a bike. There are plenty of second-hand ones around.

Are there bus lanes and cycle lanes in your town? If not, write to your local paper to suggest the idea.

Recycle as much rubbish as you can. Suggest that your house has different bins to sort paper, glass, plastics and cans.

Always buy recycled goods. They take less energy to produce.

Join a group that helps to protect the environment. Some of the groups you could try are:

Friends of the Earth *www.foe.co.uk*
Greenpeace *www.greenpeace.org.uk*

Glossary

Carbon dioxide A gas that is found in the air. Too much carbon dioxide in the air leads to global warming.

Dam A wall built across a river to stop the flow of water.

Electricity A kind of energy that flows along wires and can be used in many different ways.

Energy The power that makes machines and living things able to work. We can get energy from fuels, sunlight, water and wind.

Environment The land, air and sea that make the world around us.

Fossil fuel A fuel, such as coal, oil or gas, which formed over many millions of years from rotting animals and plants.

Fuel Wood, coal or some other material that can be burned for heat and power.

Fumes The mixture of dirt and gases that is made by burning fuel.

Gas A substance like air, which is not solid or liquid. Air is made of a mixture of different gases.

Global warming The slow warming of the Earth. It is caused by too much carbon dioxide in the air.

Material Something like wood, metal, plastic or glass that is used to make things.

Meter A machine that measures the electricity used in a house, school or other building.

Natural Found in the world around us.

Pollute To spoil the air, land or water with harmful substances.

Power station A large building where electricity is made.

Public transport Buses, trains and other vehicles that carry fare-paying passengers.

Raw material A natural material that is the starting point for making something new.

Recycle To take an old material and use it to make something new.

Solar panel A panel that uses sunlight to heat water in a house.

Wind turbine A machine that uses the power of the wind to make electricity.

Index